CELEB

SPORTS STAR

GEOFF BARKER

W
FRANKLIN WATTS
LONDON•SYDNEY

First published in 2010 by
Franklin Watts
338 Euston Road
London NW1 3BH

Franklin Watts Australia
Level 17/207 Kent Street
Sydney NSW 2000

ISBN: 978 0 7496 9262 9

Dewey classification number: 796'.092

A CIP catalogue record for this book is available from the British Library.

Planning and production by Discovery Books Limited
Managing editor: Laura Durman
Editor: Clare Hibbert
Designer: D.R. ink
Picture research: Tom Humphrey

Printed in China

Franklin Watts is a division of Hachette Children's Books, an Hachette UK company.
www.hachette.co.uk

Photo acknowledgements: Getty Images: cover (Paul Gilham), pp 4–5 (Tom Purslow), 6–7 (Glyn Kirk/AFP), 8 (Clive Brunskill), 11 (Jeff J Mitchell), 12 (Stu Forster), 13 (Adrian Dennis/ AFP), 15 (Tom Shaw), 16–17 (Phil Cole), 17 (WheelPower), 19 (Shaun Botterill), 20–21 (Francois Xavier Marit/AFP), 21 (Timothy Clary/AFP), 24–25 (Clive Mason), 25 (Quinn Rooney), 26–27 (Clive Brunskill), 28 (Hoch Zwei), 29 (Hoch Zwei); Shutterstock Images: pp 3 (sabri deniz kizil), 6 (Paul Cowan); Wikimedia Commons: pp 1 and 22–23 (Keith Allison), 18 and 31 (Karen Blaha).

Every attempt has been made to clear copyright. Should there be any inadvertent omission, please apply to the Publishers for rectification.

To the best of its knowledge, the Publisher believes the facts in this book to be true at the time of going to press. However, due to the nature of celebrity, it is impossible to guarantee that all the facts will still be current at the time of reading.

Note to parents and teachers: Every effort has been made by the Publishers to ensure that the websites in this book are suitable for children, that they are of the highest educational value, and that they contain no inappropriate or offensive material. However, because of the nature of the Internet, it is impossible to guarantee that the contents of these sites will not be altered. We strongly advise that Internet access is supervised by a responsible adult.

CONTENTS

WAYNE ROONEY

FACT

Days before his 17th birthday, Rooney scored for Everton against Arsenal, becoming the youngest goalscorer in Premier League history.

Football is one of the planet's biggest sports. Kids all over the world enjoy playing football in empty streets, parks or any patch of spare land. Huge stadiums fill to bursting with excited fans there to watch 'the beautiful game'.

SCOUSE FORCE

Everton fans knew Wayne Rooney was a star in the making when he was just a teenager. As a youngster, Rooney once scored six goals for Everton boys, including a perfect overhead kick against a Manchester United youth team. Rooney developed as a young player with Everton, then his chance came to join Manchester United in 2004.

MOVING ON UP

Wayne Rooney marked his debut for Manchester United with a stunning hat-trick against Turkish side Fenerbahce. Rooney's goal-scoring and all-round game helped his side to Premiership victory season after season.

TEMPER

Rooney is learning to cope with life in the spotlight. He is an aggressive, physical player and has been sent off several times after poor tackles. But his behaviour is steadily improving as he grows up as a footballer.

CELEB BIO

Date of birth 24 October 1985

Place of birth Croxteth, Liverpool, UK

Plays Striker

Height 1.78m

Biggest achievements Aged just 17, becoming the youngest goalscorer for England in an international match against Macedonia; winning the Premier League and the Champions League in 2007–08 with Manchester United

Inspirational figures Former Everton player, Duncan Ferguson; teammates Ryan Giggs and Paul Scholes

'I hate losing and love winning.'

Rooney celebrates after scoring a goal against Premiership rivals Arsenal.

ANDY MURRAY

Murray takes a breather at the Qatar Open.

Men's tennis is a game of firepower. Servers smash the ball down the court at up to 225 kph (140 mph) and returners have just half a second to react and guide the ball back over the net.

TALENTED TEENAGER

Andy Murray's mother coached both her tennis player sons. Andy's brother Jamie was once one of the best junior tennis players in the world – and Andy always wanted to beat his older brother. Andy moved to Barcelona aged 15 to get better tennis instruction. In 2007, at only 19, he was ranked in the world's top ten.

WHAT'S HE GOT?

Murray has a powerful serve and a brilliant double-handed backhand. He hits aggressive baseline winners even when he's in a difficult corner. And he is also one of the best at returning serves.

JUST A LITTLE BIT MORE

Murray is still looking for his first Grand Slam title – either Wimbledon or a French, Australian or US open title. In the Australian Open in 2010 he was the beaten finalist against the great Roger Federer.

HIGH HOPES

The hopes of the British public rest on Murray's shoulders. At Wimbledon in 2008, he reached the quarter-finals. He was beaten by the champion that year, Rafael Nadal. He went one better in 2009, when he was beaten in the semis by American Andy Roddick. But that same year he had briefly risen to world number two and claimed his first grass title at Queen's.

Murray playing in a Wimbledon semi-final against Andy Roddick.

CELEB BIO

Date of birth 15 May 1987

Place of birth Glasgow

Plays Right-handed player, men's singles

Height 1.90m

Biggest achievements Becoming British number one in 2006; reaching the US Open final in 2008; reaching the Australian Open final in 2010

Inspirational figures Tim Henman, Rafael Nadal

'I've beaten Federer six times and Nadal twice. The thing that's really tough to do is beat them on tennis's biggest stage.'

CELEB BIO

Name Venus Williams

Date of birth 17 June 1980

Place of birth Lynwood, California, USA

Plays Right-hander, women's singles, doubles, mixed-doubles

Height 1.85m

Biggest achievement Winning seven Grand Slam singles and 12 Grand Slam doubles

CELEB BIO

Name Serena Williams

Date of birth 26 September 1981

Place of birth Saginaw, Michigan, USA

Plays Right-hander, women's singles, doubles, mixed-doubles

Height 1.75m

Biggest achievement Winning 11 Grand Slam singles and 12 Grand Slam doubles

Venus (top) and Serena Williams (bottom) play in the women's doubles final at the Australian Open.

VENUS & SERENA WILLIAMS

Women's tennis is getting faster. Players are getting fitter and more powerful, with stronger, quicker serves. Female players have to produce all the shots in a flash because of the lightning speed of the game today.

FATHER FIGURE

Sisters Venus and Serena Williams started to play tennis when they were young. Their father was determined that at least one of them was going to be a future tennis champ. He decided to coach them himself. Little did he know that they would both become stars! Serena won the US Open in 1999 and the following year Venus won Wimbledon.

SUCCESS STORIES

Both of the Williams sisters have been incredibly successful. As two of the top women's singles players, the sisters have had to play against each other. Serena has won six of their eight Grand Slam encounters.

FIGHTING FOR RIGHTS

Until recently, women tennis players were paid less prize money than the men. Venus Williams fought hard for equal pay and eventually won her campaign. Tennis prize money is now the same for men and women. Venus was the first player to benefit from equal pay when she became 2007 Wimbledon Champion.

ROLE MODELS

Both Venus and Serena are great role models. They came from a poor neighbourhood in Los Angeles, USA, but their hard work and dedication have brought them celebrity and success. Venus became the first UNESCO Promoter of Gender Equality in 2006.

'I believe that athletes – especially female athletes in the world's leading sport for women – should serve as role models.' VENUS

'I think it's just built within you that you... want to better yourself and you want to play the game that you love.'

BRIAN O'DRISCOLL

Rugby union is a tough, physical game played between two teams of 15 players. Like all sportsmen and women, rugby players need mental strength and skill, as well as a burning desire to win.

TRUE HERO

Brian O'Driscoll plays outside centre for Leinster and Ireland, as well as the British and Irish Lions team. This modest, likeable superstar is one of the greats. One of his biggest triumphs was leading Ireland to victory in the 2009 Six Nations tournament. Ireland defeated all five other teams to achieve a very rare Grand Slam victory – Ireland's first since 1948.

EARLY YEARS

As a boy, O'Driscoll was a football fan. He did not really play rugby until he was about 12, when he went to a rugby-playing school called Blackrock College in Dublin. O'Driscoll came from a family of successful rugby players – his father and two uncles all played rugby for Ireland.

PRESENCE ON THE PITCH

O'Driscoll first played for Ireland in 1999 aged 20. He became captain in 2003. Totally committed, O'Driscoll is a huge presence on the rugby field. He plays with guts, fearlessly tackles players bigger than himself and shows his leadership qualities by driving his side on.

LOVE OF RUGBY

O'Driscoll is passionate about the game. 'I love going out every day and training and being part of the team,' he says. Training and dedication are very important, but O'Driscoll just lives for the game of rugby.

CELEB BIO

Date of birth 21 January 1979

Place of birth Clontarf, Dublin, Ireland

Plays Outside centre for Leinster, Ireland and British and Irish Lions

Height 1.77m

Biggest achievements Being chosen as Player of the Tournament in the Six Nations in 2006, 2007 and 2009

Inspirational figure Richie McCaw from the New Zealand All Blacks

O'Driscoll lifts the Heineken Cup after his side, Leinster, beat Leicester Tigers.

CHRISTINE OHURUOGU

Ohuruogu competing for Team GB in the 400m at the World Athletics Championships.

Track-and-field athletics involve running, throwing or jumping in competition with other athletes. Runners compete to be the quickest over a certain distance. Win gold at the Olympics and you're the best in the world.

EXPLOSIVE SPRINTER

Christine Ohuruogu is a British sprinter. She is an explosive runner over short distances of 60, 100 and also 200 metres. But 400 metres is her real strength. Other athletes may start faster over the longer distance of 400 metres, but thanks to her pace as a sprinter, Ohuruogu often finishes very strongly.

A PERSONAL BATTLE

Christine Ohuruogu has had her problems. In 2006 she missed three compulsory drugs tests and was suspended from racing. Ohuruogu threatened to quit running for Britain, and compete for another country. At the end of 2007, Ohuruogu was declared innocent of taking drugs. Free to compete for Team GB at the 2008 Olympics, Ohuruogu had just a few months to get ready.

A WINNER

The Beijing 2008 Olympics was a momentous time for Christine Ohuruogu. In the 400 metres final, she rounded the bend into the last 100 metres in fifth place. Amazingly, she powered past everyone, including US rival Sanya Richards, to win with a time of 49.62 seconds. Ohuruogu had just won the gold medal for Britain.

Ohuruogu with her Olympic gold medal in Beijing.

CELEB BIO

Date of birth **17 May 1984**

Place of birth **London**

Events **400m, 4x400m relay**

Height **1.75m**

Biggest achievement **Winning Britain's only track-and-field gold medal at the Beijing 2008 Olympics**

Inspirational figure **Her old PE teacher**

'I think you can become a better and stronger person through athletics.'

KEVIN PIETERSEN

Cricket is often a war of nerves. The fortune of a side can quickly turn, first one way, then the other. Some cricketers make the game even more exciting, adding flair and daring to their great skill and technique.

HARD-HITTER

Kevin Pietersen, or KP for short, is one of the most thrilling talents in the game of cricket. This attacking right-handed batsman likes to dominate bowlers, scoring runs quickly. A hard-hitter, he oozes confidence at the crease. Pietersen has an aggressive, swashbuckling style of play that is a joy to watch.

TEST DEBUT

Born in South Africa, Pietersen has an English mother. He now lives in England and plays cricket for Hampshire as well as the English national side. In 2005 Pietersen made his Test debut for England against Australia. This was the year of a historic English Ashes victory. During the fifth and final Test, KP made an amazing match-saving innings of 158. Pietersen soon became England's top batsman, with an impressive Test average of 50. In 2009 Pietersen was part of the victorious English side that beat Australia in the Ashes, although he took part in only the first two Tests as he had to undergo surgery on his Achilles tendon.

MODERN SUPERSTAR

Today, Pietersen is one of cricket's biggest stars. He was paid $1.5 million per year to play in the Indian Premier League (IPL). Like many superstars, he is married to a fellow celebrity – singer Jessica Taylor. He has famous friends too. The best man at his wedding was ex-England teammate and former *Strictly Come Dancing* champion, Darren Gough.

CELEB BIO

Date of birth **27 June 1980**

Place of birth **Pietermaritzburg, Natal, South Africa**

Plays **Batsman for Hampshire, England and Royal Challengers Bangalore; also bowls**

Height **1.93m**

Biggest achievement **Helping England to win the Ashes in 2005 and finishing the series as top scorer**

Inspirational figures **Former cricketers Shaun Pollock and Errol Stewart**

'Discipline is good. It taught me that I didn't always have to have what I wanted.'

Pietersen playing in a Test match for England against Australia.

ADE ADEPITAN

'[Sport's] taught me discipline, helped me to become focused, given me goals in life and taken me all over the world.'

CELEB BIO

Date of birth **27 March 1973**

Place of birth **Lagos, Nigeria**

Plays **International wheelchair basketball; in training for wheelchair tennis**

Biggest achievement **Bronze medal in Athens 2004 Paralympics**

Inspirational figures **His mum and dad**

Adepitan appeals for new sports wheelchairs, on behalf of the charity WheelPower.

Basketball is one of the world's most popular sports. The first game of wheelchair basketball was played in 1946 by a group of disabled US World War II veterans. Today it is estimated that more than 100,000 people play this fast-moving sport.

WORKING HARD

Ade Adepitan survived polio at the age of six months, but the disease left him unable to walk. At first he used calipers, but he preferred the wheelchair as it was quicker. He soon developed a strong upper body and arms. Sports doctors persuaded Adepitan to enter the Junior Wheelchair Games.

WINNING GOLD

After playing the sport for almost 14 years, Adepitan was chosen for the British wheelchair basketball team. He went on to represent Britain in two Paralympic Games. He won a bronze medal in Athens in 2004, then struck gold in the Paralympic World Cup in Manchester in 2005.

MOTIVATOR

Adepitan has become a well-known face on television as a presenter and commentator. He also starred in *Desperados*, a children's TV drama about wheelchair basketball. Adepitan spends a lot of time travelling around schools. He does energetic wheelchair basketball demos to encourage kids to get involved with sports. At the same time, he raises awareness about disability – and what people can achieve with the right attitude. In 2005 he received an MBE for his services to disabled sports.

Adepitan (centre) and Simon Munn (right) take on Italy's Fabio Raimondi (left) in the Paralympics wheelchair basketball quarter-final.

FACT

Following on from his success at basketball, Ade Adepitan is planning a totally new sports career. He is in training for the 2012 Paralympics, this time playing wheelchair tennis.

'I don't want to lose. That's the thing. If I don't want to lose, I can focus.'

MICHAEL PHELPS

Swimmers compete with each other over a set distance in all types of strokes, including breaststroke, backstroke and freestyle. A swimmer rarely manages to win more than two or three different events, but American swimmer Michael Phelps has won eight separate events!

HEAPS OF ENERGY

Michael Phelps was diagnosed as having Attention Deficit Hyperactivity Disorder (ADHD) at an early age. He found it hard to concentrate and was often fidgety and restless. He found swimming a useful way to burn off some of his extra energy. By the age of ten, it was clear to his coach that he was a great swimming talent.

GOLD!

Phelps has dominated the sport of swimming at the very highest level. His achievements at the 2004 Athens Olympics were amazing – he won six gold and two bronze medals. Four years later, he went to Beijing and won eight more golds!

SPECIAL FOCUS

To win his eight gold medals at the 2008 Olympics, Phelps set seven new world records and one Olympic record. He did not appear to suffer from nerves at all. He had a special focus, which he said came from his ADHD. During each race he thought about nothing but touching the wall first, before the other swimmers.

Phelps after winning the men's 100m butterfly final at the Athens Olympics.

CELEB BIO

Date of birth **30 June 1985**

Place of birth **Baltimore, Maryland, USA**

Strokes **Butterfly, individual medley, freestyle, backstroke**

Height **1.93m**

Biggest achievements **Winning 14 gold medals – more than any other Olympian; being named World Swimmer of the Year many times over**

Inspiration **Bob Bowman, Phelps' coach since the age of 11**

REBECCA ADLINGTON

Swimming is all about pushing your body to the limits to see how fast you can swim. Swimmers have to go flat out to win – and that means practising the race, as fast as possible, over and over again.

DOUBLE GOLD

British swimmer Rebecca Adlington won two gold medals at the 2008 Beijing Olympics. She pipped America's Katie Hoff in the 400-metre freestyle, and easily won the 800-metre freestyle with a record time of 8:14.10. She was six seconds ahead of the silver medallist, Italy's Alessia Filippi. Adlington had also smashed US swimming star Janet Evans' 19-year record by two seconds.

IN PEAK SHAPE

Adlington began swimming at the age of four and was competing at ten. She joined the Nova Centurion Swimming Club in 2001, where Bill Furniss became her coach. He makes sure she is in peak shape for big competitions. As a result of years of hard training, focus and complete dedication to the sport, Adlington has made it to the very top.

RECORD BREAKER

Adlington has broken all sorts of swimming records. At Beijing 2008, she was the first British woman to win an Olympic swimming gold in nearly 50 years. She was also the first British swimmer to win more than one gold medal at a single Olympic Games since Henry Taylor – a century earlier.

'I don't feel like a world-record holder. I just feel like a normal girl.'

Adlington on the winners' podium at the Beijing Olympics, after coming first in the women's 400m freestyle.

CELEB BIO

Date of birth **17 February 1989**

Place of birth **Mansfield, Nottinghamshire**

Events **400m and 800m freestyle; 200m and relay**

Height **1.79m**

Biggest achievement **Winning two Olympic golds**

FACT

Rebecca Adlington spends around 20 gruelling hours a week swimming. That means she has already spent over one whole year of her life in the pool!

Adlington competing in the 400m women's freestyle.

TIGER WOODS

Golf has been around since the 18th century. It is only in recent years that it has become hugely popular – with all sorts of people. One star has done more than anyone else to make golf into the sport it is today. His name is Tiger Woods.

EARLY STARTER

American professional golfer Eldrick 'Tiger' Woods started playing golf at a young age. According to legend, he was swinging a sawn-off golf club at the age of 11 months and began to play when he was two. He went on to win the Junior World Championships six times.

WORLD NUMBER ONE

Woods became a professional golfer in 1996, immediately receiving $40 million (around £24 million) for promoting Nike products. Recognized as the world's best golfer, in 2008 Woods earned $110 million (around £65 million) in prizes and sponsorship money – making him the highest-paid professional athlete in the world.

PRACTICE MAKES PERFECT

Woods aims for perfection in his golf, putting in hard work and endless practice. He has an excellent all-round game, able to make long drives from the tee and also putt well under pressure. Thanks to his natural ability and determination, he has spent over ten years at the very top of the game.

UNDER PRESSURE

Tiger Woods had to face his toughest test in 2009 after a scandal rocked his personal life and threatened his marriage. Woods gave up golfing for a while. Like many celebrities before him, he will have to rebuild his life – very much in the public eye.

CELEB BIO

Date of birth **30 December 1975**

Place of birth **Cypress, California, USA**

Height **1.85m**

Biggest achievements **Winning 14 golf majors and being made Professional Golfers' Association (PGA) Player of the Year a record nine times**

Inspirational figure **His father, Earl Woods**

'No matter how good you get, you can always get better and that's the exciting part.'

FACT
Woods rose to number one in the Official World Golf Rankings before the end of his first professional year – the fastest ever rise to the top!

CHRIS HOY

Hoy in action during a 1-km time trial.

FACT

Chris Hoy became Sports Personality of the Year in 2008. He gained a huge 40 per cent of the public vote.

The first cycle race took place about 150 years ago. The competitors raced on wooden bicycles with iron tyres. Today, bikes are much lighter and faster. Athletes ride at speeds of up to 75 kph (47 mph) on banked tracks in purpose-built velodromes.

TRACK CYCLING

Chris Hoy is an inspirational track cyclist from Edinburgh. He has been active in sports from an early age, representing Scotland as a junior in rowing as well as BMX racing.

COPING WITH CHANGE

At the 2004 Olympics in Athens, Hoy claimed gold in the Kilo, the one-kilometre time trial. The following year, the International Cycling Union (UCI) removed the event. Hoy had to recover from this setback and find a new speciality. He chose the Keirin, an event where sprinters race flat out for 600 to 700 metres after a paced start behind a motorbike.

THE FLYING SCOTSMAN

At the Beijing Olympics in 2008, Hoy led Team GB to victory, demonstrating his immense sprinting power and determination. He won three gold medals (for the individual sprint, team sprint and Keirin) and became the first British Olympian in 100 years to win a treble in the same games. In 2009, the Queen knighted him for his services to cycling, and he became Sir Chris Hoy.

Hoy shows off his three gold medals at the Beijing Olympics.

CELEB BIO

Date of birth **23 March 1976**

Place of birth **Edinburgh**

Events **Kilo, sprint cycling (track), Keirin**

Height **1.86m**

Biggest achievement **Winning three golds in the 2008 Beijing Olympics**

Inspirational figure **Scottish cyclist Graeme Obree**

'I try to go into a race with a frame of mind that I couldn't have trained harder. So I take the pressure off myself and know that I'm in the best possible shape.'

Check out Chris Hoy's official website www.chrishoy.com

BETH TWEDDLE

'I started gymnastics when I was seven because I had too much energy around the house. I was always jumping on beds, [and] climbing trees...'

Tweddle competing on the uneven bars for Team GB at the Olympics.

FACT

The uneven bars, also called the asymmetric bars, are a piece of equipment used only by female gymnasts. Male gymnasts compete on the high bar and parallel bars.

CELEB BIO

Date of birth **1 April 1985**

Place of birth **Johannesburg, South Africa**

Events **Uneven bars and floor exercise**

Height **1.59m**

Biggest achievement **Gymnastics world champion on uneven bars in 2006 and on the floor event in 2009**

Inspirational figures **Athletes Kelly Holmes and Sally Gunnell**

Gymnastics is an exciting sport for athletes who are fit, flexible, agile and focused. Strong but graceful gymnasts make daring jumps and flips on various pieces of equipment, including the parallel bars, balance beam and vault.

BEST OF BRITISH

Beth Tweddle is the most successful British gymnast of all time. Her first international competition was the 2001 Gymnastics' World Championships, when she was just 16. Five years later she won Britain's first-ever gymnastics gold medal at the 2006 World Championships in Denmark with a high score (16.200 points) in the uneven bars event.

HIGH AND LOW BARS

Tweddle's main event of uneven bars consists of two parallel bars of different heights. The gymnast mounts the bars, performs a routine, then dismounts at the end. The gymnast performs swings to build up speed and launches herself from one bar to the other. She tries to achieve perfect technique.

CAREER HIGHS AND LOWS

Beth Tweddle really came to the public's attention at the Beijing Olympics in 2008. She bravely attempted a very difficult bars routine and narrowly missed out on a bronze medal. At the 2009 World Championships, Tweddle fell in her preferred bars routine. She recovered to win gold in the floor event – a routine performed to music that includes handstands, tumbling and other acrobatics. Now that she is both world and European number one in floor gymnastics, Tweddle is aiming for gold in the 2012 London Olympics.

FACT

Lewis Hamilton was named after the famous American sprinter and long jumper Carl Lewis.

'When you're not winning you've got to dig deep... to get yourself back up there.'

LEWIS HAMILTON

Hamilton with Nicole Scherzinger of the Pussycat Dolls.

With drivers racing at speeds of up to 360 kph (225 mph), Formula One is an exciting sport. Drivers need skill, desire and guts. It is a turbo-charged, glamorous world, but it takes dedication and a great deal of effort to make it to the top.

JUST WATCH ME GO

Lewis Hamilton got a go-kart from his father at the age of six. He began racing go-karts two years later. When he was only ten, the determined young boy introduced himself to Ron Dennis, the McLaren team principal. Hamilton had just won the British Karting Championship and told Dennis he wanted to race for him one day. Hamilton went on to develop his skills through car racing – he was champion in Formula Renault, Formula Three and then GP2. Hamilton became a McLaren Mercedes Formula One (F1) driver in 2007.

WHAT A START!

Lewis Hamilton became a superstar in his first season of F1 motor racing. He finished second in the 2007 F1 Championship with 12 podium finishes, including four wins. Although he was a rookie driver (a newcomer to the sport), Hamilton finished only one point behind that year's champion, Finland's Kimi Raikkonen.

CHAMPION

The following year, Hamilton won five races and had a further five podium finishes for a total of 98 points. At the age of only 23 years, 8 months and 26 days, he became the youngest F1 World Champion. Although Hamilton made a disappointing start in 2009, he improved in the second half of the season, winning the Hungarian and Singapore Grands Prix.

WORLD OF GLAMOUR

Hamilton enjoys the flashy side of F1. He has dated a string of glamorous women, including singer Natasha Bedingfield, former Miss Great Britain Danielle Lloyd and Pussycat Dolls' singer Nicole Scherzinger. But Hamilton is always focused foremost on F1.

CELEB BIO

Date of birth **7 January 1985**

Place of birth **Stevenage, Hertfordshire, UK**

Height **1.74m**

Biggest achievements **Winning in his second F1 Championship season; being awarded an MBE in 2009**

Inspirational figure **F1 racing driver, Ayrton Senna**

aggressive In sport, bold and energetic.

agile Quick and light in movement.

arm span The total length of a person's outstretched arms, from the tip of the fingers of one hand to the those of the other.

Attention Deficit Hyperactivity Disorder (ADHD) A disorder that can mean a child finds it hard to concentrate or to control his or her behaviour. ADHD can sometimes continue into adulthood.

baseline In tennis, the white line at the back of the court that divides the 'in' and 'out' areas.

BMX Short for 'bicycle motocross'; a type of stunt riding over obstacles on specially-designed bikes.

calipers Leg braces used by polio survivors or other people with walking disabilities.

crease Short for popping crease. In cricket, white lines that mark the area where a batsman must stand.

dismount To get off.

drive In golf, when a golfer hits a big first shot towards a hole.

golf majors The world's top four golfing tournaments: the Masters Tournament, the US Open, the Open Championship and the PGA Championship.

GP2 A stepping-stone car series for drivers aiming to compete in Formula One (F1). The racing cars look like F1 cars, but are much slower.

Grand Slam A special sporting achievement. In tennis, winning a Grand Slam means being champion at one of the world's top four competitions: the French Open, Wimbledon, the US Open or the Australian Open. In rugby, winning a Grand Slam means beating all the other sides in the same year during the Six Nations Championships (or earlier versions of the competition).

hat-trick Scoring a treble, such as three goals in a match or three matches in a row in a competition.

innings In cricket, the period when one team is batting; a batsman also plays an innings.

mount To get on to.

Olympic Games A four-yearly international sporting event, hosted by a different city each time.

parallel bars Gymnastic bars used by male gymnasts that are a set distance from one another at the same height.

Paralympic Games A four-yearly international sporting event for athletes with disabilities, held immediately after the Olympic Games and at the same venue.

podium finish In motor racing, coming first, second or third, and therefore taking a place on the winners' podium (or platform).

polio A serious disease that can leave someone unable to walk or use their arms.

professional Describes someone who does something – for example, sport – for a living, rather than unpaid and just for fun.

putt In golf, to make a shot on the golfing green with a flat club called a putter.

rookie A sportsperson in his or her first year.

six In cricket, the highest score a batsman can make in a single stroke, for example with a big hit over the boundary.

sponsorship Promotion of a company or its products in return for money. Many sportsmen and women earn more from sponsorship deals than they do from prize winnings.

technique Special skills developed by a sportsman or woman to become a better player or athlete.

Test In cricket, the longest version of a match between countries, lasting up to five days.

UNESCO Short for United Nations Educational, Scientific and Cultural Organization, an agency that sponsors projects to promote cooperation between different countries.

uneven bars Gymnastic bars used by female gymnasts that are a set distance from one another at different or uneven heights.

velodrome Purpose-built cycle track with steep, banked sides.

FURTHER INFORMATION

BOOKS

21st Century Lives: British Olympians by Debbie Foy (Wayland, 2009)

21st Century Lives: Sports People by Liz Gogerly (Wayland, 2004)

DK Eyewitness: Olympics by Chris Oxlade (Dorling Kindersley, 2005)

Dream to Win: Andy Murray by Roy Apps (Franklin Watts, 2009)

Dream to Win: Chris Hoy by Roy Apps (Franklin Watts, 2009)

Dream to Win: Rebecca Adlington by Roy Apps (Franklin Watts, 2009)

Dream to Win: Tiger Woods by Roy Apps (Franklin Watts, 2010)

Dream to Win: Wayne Rooney by Roy Apps (Franklin Watts, 2010)

The Story of the Olympics by Minna Lacey (Usborne Publishing Ltd, 2008)

DVDS

Lewis Hamilton: Life in the Fast Lane (Warner Music Entertainment, 2008)

The Olympic Series: Golden Moments 1920 to 2002 (Paramount Home Entertainment, 2004)

Rooney: My First Year at Manchester United (2 Entertain Video, 2005)

Wimbledon The 2008 Men's Final – Nadal v Federer (Target DVD, 2008)

Wimbledon The 2009 Men's Final – Federer v Roddick (Good Guys Media Ltd, 2009)

WEBSITES

http://news.bbc.co.uk/sport
Comprehensive news and statistics on all your favourite sports.

http://uk.eurosport.yahoo.com/
Follow your favourite sports, read the expert blogs or create your fantasy football or F1 team.

http://www.metro.co.uk/sport
Up-to-date news and views in newspaper sports page format.

http://www.olympics.org.uk/home2.aspx
The website of the British Olympic Association with news of Team GB athletes.

INDEX